Women Like Me

Embracing the Unseen - The Courage to Surrender

Special Anniversary Edition

Julie Fairhurst

Compiled by Julie Fairhurst
Copyright Julie Fairhurst 2023 – Rock Star Publishing
Paperback Edition: ISBN: 978-1-990639-18-0
Hardcover Edition: ISBN 978-1-990639-19-7
Interior & Cover Design by STOKE Publishing

The authors of this book do not dispense medical advice or prescribe the use of any technique as a form of treatment for physical, emotional, or medical problems without a physician's advice, either directly or indirectly. The authors intend to provide general information to individuals taking positive steps in their lives for emotional and spiritual well-being. If you use any information in this book for yourself, which is your constitutional right, the authors and the publishers assume no responsibility for your actions.

At times, some readers may be triggered by a women's story. Should you need to speak with someone, there are many crisis lines, counselors, and doctors that you can reach out to. Find someone who can lend a kind ear to listen to you. That can be a friend, parent, spouse, or anyone you trust. Your local community services may have telephone numbers to assist you.

Contents

Part Two
Women Like Me Movement

"Something amazing happens when we surrender and just love. We melt into another world, a realm of power already within us. The world changes when we change. The world softens when we soften. The world loves us when we choose to love the world."

Marianne Williamson

Special Anniversary Edition

Welcome to the Special Anniversary Edition of the "Women Like Me" Chapter Books, a milestone celebration of a decade of inspiration, empowerment, and profound storytelling. As we embark on this special journey, we pay tribute to the incredible women who have graced the pages of our past nine volumes. Their voices, stories, and wisdom have woven a rich tapestry of experiences that have resonated with readers worldwide.

Since 2019, "Women Like Me" has become more than just a collection of books; it has evolved into a powerful movement, a testament to women's strength, resilience, and creativity from all walks of life. Through these pages, we have celebrated triumphs and explored the depths of adversity, sharing personal stories about womanhood's diverse and intricate facets.

In this special anniversary edition, we honor and express our deepest gratitude to every writer who has contributed their words, insights, and hearts to the "Women Like Me" series. Each writer has added a unique brushstroke to our collective masterpiece, painting a vivid portrait of the myriad experiences that make up the world of women.

Whether you were with us from the very beginning or joined us along the way, your words have made an indelible mark on our readers' lives, and for that, we are profoundly thankful.

As we celebrate this milestone, you are invited to reacquaint yourself with our powerful authors who have graced our pages. These authors remind us of the strength from vulnerability, the courage found in adversity, and the beauty that emerges from the tapestry of shared experiences.

It is a testament to the ever-evolving nature of the "Women Like Me" community—a community that continues to grow, inspire, and uplift, just as it has since 2019.

So, as we embark on this journey through the heart and soul of "Women Like Me," we celebrate not only the past but also the future —the stories yet to be told, the voices yet to be heard, and the endless possibilities that lie ahead. Thank you for being a part of our remarkable journey, and here's to the next ten books of inspiration, empowerment, and the enduring legacy of "Women Like Me."

"We are at our most powerful the moment
we no longer need to be powerful."

Eric Michael Leventhal

Introduction

In our modern world, characterized by noise, incessant demands, and perpetual motion, surrender often seems like a distant, elusive ideal. It's a notion that can feel out of reach, especially in a society that prizes control and constant activity. Yet, for women, surrendering to the unseen can be a powerful and transformative journey of self-discovery, empowerment, and spiritual awakening.

It's time to redefine surrender and transcend the stereotypes and misconceptions surrounding it. Surrender is not about giving up or admitting defeat. Rather, it's about embracing the unknown, trusting in the process, and opening oneself to new possibilities and experiences.

The term "surrender" often carries a multitude of meanings and emotions. For some, it evokes images of weakness or submission; for others, it represents a profound release from the burdens of control and perfectionism. However, surrender takes on a new, empowering dimension in the context of personal growth and self-discovery.

Surrender, in this sense, becomes a powerful tool for personal transformation. It is about letting go of the need to control every aspect of our lives and instead trusting in our innate wisdom and the unseen forces that guide us. It is about embracing the unknown and the unseen and finding strength and wisdom.

Often misunderstood, surrender is not about giving up or losing control. It's about recognizing the limits of our human perspective and opening ourselves up to the vast wisdom of the universe. It's about acknowledging that forces in our lives are beyond our control and understanding. And it's about learning to trust these forces, to let them guide us, and to surrender to their wisdom.

Embark on a journey of profound exploration into the heart of surrender. This is not a tale of relinquishing control but an invitation to understand that forces are at play beyond our immediate perception. This story is about tapping into a source of profound strength and wisdom by letting go.

There is a profound strength to be found in surrender. When we stop trying to control everything and let go of our need for certainty and our fear of the unknown, we open ourselves up to new possibilities. We tap into a source of wisdom and strength that is far greater than our own. We become more resilient, adaptable, and able to navigate life's challenges.

This journey of surrender is not an easy one. It requires courage, patience, and a willingness to face our fears. But the rewards are immense. As we learn to let go and trust in the universe's wisdom, we find a sense of peace and contentment beyond anything we could have imagined. We discover an unshakeable strength within ourselves, a profound wisdom, and an unending joy.

Surrender can be a path to profound liberation. It's about breaking free from the constraints that hold us back, from the fears and anxieties that keep us tethered to the familiar. By surrendering, we can discover new facets of ourselves, unlock our potential, and step into a more authentic, empowered version of ourselves.

To explore the unknown, face your fears, and discover the profound strength and wisdom within you. It's a journey that will help transform your life and lead you to a deeper understanding of yourself and the world around you. And it's a journey that begins with a single step: the step of surrender.

So we invite you, dear reader, to embark on this journey of surrender. To explore the art of surrender and to discover what it means to let go truly. It's a journey that promises personal growth and self-discovery, a deeper connection to the world around us, and a renewed sense of purpose and meaning.

Julie Fairhurst

Founder of Women Like Me

Part One

Women Like Me

Embracing the Unseen - The Courage to Surrender

"To get over the past, you first have to accept that the past is over. No matter how many times you revisit it, analyze it, regret it, or sweat it...it's over. It can hurt you no more."

Mandy Hale

Chapter 1

Accepting The Challenge Allowed Healing To Occur

Joanne Smith

"Change is the essence of life; be willing to surrender what you are for what you could become."
Reinhold Niebuhr

In February 2022, my therapist and I were reading the book 'The Body Keeps the Score.' It was like the author of this book had sat in my childhood living room and watched as the trauma played out. Our session that day was very intense. It brought me back to a time I didn't want to visit. Bringing up the feelings associated with enduring the abuse I had no control over made me feel very vulnerable.

As a child, I used to believe that the bruises left on my upper arms from being shaken or restrained were my fault. My dad would say, "If you didn't fight so hard to get away, it wouldn't be so bad." I was never told to cover up the fly swatter welts on the inside of my legs or the handprint bruises on my upper arms. I just knew to do it. I didn't want anyone to think I was a 'bad girl'...because that is what I was told, so it must have been true. I wasn't sure how I felt about hiding what was happening to me.

I didn't know if any of my friends at school were getting hit or if it was just me. I was making my own way in this world, unprotected and unseen. It was scary as hell! I knew treating my children like this would not be okay, so I made it my life's mission to do just the opposite with my own children.

I was paying attention to other family dynamics in the people around me ...and taking mental notes. My therapist and I talked about what it would have been like to have had someone to talk to about how I felt after a traumatic experience. She asked: 'If I could imagine going back and talking to my 'five-year-old self,' what might I say to comfort her?'

It was mentally exhausting to think about how my situation would have been different had I had someone to hold me and tell me everything would be ok. Perhaps if I could see my five-year-old self being comforted, the trauma wouldn't feel so real now.

Knowing my best arsenal at the time in dealing with painful memories was to write poetry, I had the following homework assignment in my inbox when I got home from that session.

1) Write a poem that draws a picture of you holding five-year-old Joanne and describe what you can offer her.

2) If you are in a situation, imagine holding and comforting her.

I have to admit, I thought the assignment was a little lame. I couldn't understand it on Wednesday, Thursday, and most of Friday. When I tried to get into my five-year-old self's mind frame, I only felt fear, helplessness, and anxiety. How would I turn these feelings into something soothing to a little girl?

But after giving it much thought, things started to shift. I was a little annoyed at my therapist for a while until I figured it out. But after writing the poem, I thought I should trust her more often. By accepting the challenge, I allowed healing to occur.

The poem I wrote is called 'Warrior Princess.'

Feb 12/22 - To my 5-Year-old Self:

Warrior Princess

A picture is worth a thousand words,
And your precious little smile tells a story,
It hides the senseless act of much abuse,
And for that I am so truly sorry.

You were scared and had no one to talk to,
Your own mother would even look away,
Helpless to the distress that consumed you,
You became compliant, forced to obey.

Climb up on my lap little angel,
I'll hold you until you don't shake,
You're a warrior, dressed as a princess,
I'll stay with you until you awake.

We'll cuddle together and tell stories,
You can trust me to be your friend,
I'll show you that tenderness exists,
And that your fear and anxiety will mend.

The strength that you'll need to get through this,
I pray that you'll see it in my eyes,
A place that is safe and so peaceful,
So that promise and faith will give rise.

So when you're feeling particularly broken,
Remember the time that we shared,

So you'll feel loved, excepted and soothed,
It will help you to feel better prepared.

Love,
Your 60-Year-old Self

Writing this poem made me realize how far I had come from that scared and hopeless little girl. Writing it felt cleansing. I could understand better now how afraid I felt as a child, not having emotional support from a caregiver, and that my fears and feelings of helplessness were real emotions, not just something I got through or had to hide.

Considering my home situation and the disconnection I felt from the world I lived in then, I could now recognize these feelings, knowing they were warranted. By surrendering to the fear and hopelessness I felt as my five-year-old self, I was allowed to focus on my strengths and the courage it took to process this tragedy.

Not being angry with myself for being unable to manage situations perfectly gave me a new perspective I can use moving forward. The courage I found to write this poem lets me know I can overcome the worst aspects of my life!

My Warrior Princess allowed me to see that I was letting go of someone I inherently am not...that scared little girl who had no one to reach out to for support, and that good things are coming because I'm stronger now and am creating what I've always wanted...a safe and secure environment to grow in. I'm shifting my focus. In shifting my focus with a more positive outlook, I can think less of the past and more about who I am in the present.

"At fifteen, life had taught me undeniably that surrender, in its place, was as honorable as resistance, especially if one had no choice."

Maya Angelou

Chapter 2

The Magic Of Healing Belief

Sabrina Lambert

"Too often, we underestimate the power of a touch, a smile, a kind word, a listening ear, an honest compliment, or the smallest act of caring, all of which have the potential to turn a life around."
Leo Buscaglia

"I will not take chemo again!" My dear friend was emphatic. "I don't care what the doctor says. I am not doing it!" He had just returned from an appointment with his specialist, and a year had passed since his surgery and the last of six months' worth of seizure-causing chemo treatments so nasty that they left him with a broken wrist and sweat-pouring tremors.

Now, a new lump had grown rapidly over a couple of months in his throat, entangled around his vocal cords and large enough to be visible on the outside of his neck. The appointment was to have a new biopsy.

I could see the fear in his eyes. He was not fearing the disease that may be taking another foothold in his body, but that he would have to experience the pain and sickness that he had originally experienced during the first round of diagnosed treatments.

"So, what's the plan then?" I tried to keep my own fear that his cancer was returning under wraps. I was secretly afraid that if he was not willing to re-experience the standard treatment, I might actually lose him.

"What will you do if the test comes back positive?" I mustered as much calm to sound caring and inquisitive to what his alternative might be instead of chemo treatments. "I don't know. I am hoping that it is nothing," he said. Reaching out, I held his hand and replied, "You don't sound like you are convinced; I don't think the doctor would have taken a biopsy if he wasn't concerned about it. Would you rather wait and worry about the prognosis, or would you want to do something that may set you up to be better prepared for whatever the next step is?"

We talked for the rest of the afternoon about how, even though it might be too early to dismiss chemo as a possible treatment, maybe we could be looking for an alternative that he could be more willing to try. To be proactive and get his body ready to heal.

My friend was living in my parent's home, house-sitting while they traveled. I lived and worked a province away and had access to the local Cancer Agency Library, so I offered to research a detoxifying tea I had read about.

The research information at the library was extensive and indicated many positive outcomes from many types of disease. I checked locally, and one health food and supplement store carried a tea with ingredients similar to the one in the research.

On my next visit back home, I brought some with me for my friend to try. It tasted like licking tree bark and horrible stuff, but only a few ounces of the tea was required per day. He agreed that it would be better to do something rather than nothing, and taking the tea to help his body detox and work on healing itself was how he saw it working.

He had been taking the supplement for about two weeks when the biopsy came back positive, and the doctor wanted to admit my friend immediately into the hospital for surgery. However, the surgeon was not able to guarantee that my friend's vocal cords or voice would survive the surgery.

This was the straw that my friend used to refuse the surgery and promised that he would come back in eight weeks to be rechecked. He strongly believed that the tea was helping, and if nothing changed at that time, he would do what the doctor recommended. Of course, the specialist protested, but my friend was determined to let his chosen remedy have a chance to do its magic.

Although I was filled with angst for him and for myself at the thought of losing my friend, and even though I did not necessarily agree with his choice, it was still his choice not to follow the standard treatment procedures when he had had such horrendous experiences with it in the past.

I learned then that caregiving can be more than the actual physical caretaking of a person. It is more important to listen to the person, learn their reasons for their choices, and support them because it helps make their belief in their choice valid and powerful. I know that belief is powerful, and especially when it comes to healing, belief in what you are doing to get better is just as powerful; I have seen it with my own eyes and my dear friend's experience.

Two months later, he did return to see the specialist. The specialist expected to biopsy the growth again, but was completely surprised that there was no growth left in my friend's throat from which to take any sample. Of course the doctor was curious about what my friend had done and was very happy that my friend was now completely clear.

We celebrated the magic that day, then celebrated it again on our wedding day a couple of years later, and we continue to celebrate this magic of healing belief going on for more than 30 years.

"Don't despair: despair suggests you are in total control and know what is coming. You don't - surrender to events with hope."

Alain de Botton

Chapter 3

Life Is Short. Life Is Precious

Lisa Kalinski

"If you change the way you look at things,
the things you look at change."
Wayne Dyer

I have a magic bench on a hill in my yard. Yes, I literally have one. I almost refer to it daily in general conversations with people. It sits on the hill overlooking my yard and the valley below. It is a special place where I sit on beautiful days, admire my surroundings, think about life, and enjoy a glass of wine.

I can hear you asking, why is it magic?

To me, it is a place of manifestation. I share this special place with my friends and when it comes up in conversation, random visitors too. It is a comforting place and has been especially powerful for those seeking love.

Let's say I have had a few successes for those who took the time to conjure up their ideal partner on this bench, put it on paper, and give it to the universe. This rickety old bench lights up my heart for some reason, and it's my favorite place to sit with my thoughts.

Sometimes it's tears, laughter, and many times hopes and dreams. This bench has given me so many great sits already. It might sound silly, but marriages have been made here too. It is no coincidence. For this bench to truly serve you, you must have an innate sense of trust in the unseen. Just like driving at night, you can only see as far as you can see. You must trust that the road will unfold in front of you, and as you keep going, keep trusting until you arrive at your destination.

If I have crappy thoughts, I sit on my bench and replace them with good thoughts. Teach your mind only to think and process the good stuff. Just let that other shit go.

My screensaver reminds me that I am powerful, whole, harmonious, and happy. Today, that is my mantra. I can't argue with that. I am all of those things.

I found my own Mr. Right using this technique, and I couldn't quite believe it when he appeared in my life. We regularly sit on the bench, reminiscing about our life together and how far we have come.

Before I found my Mr. Right, I actually had a break-up system when it came to fizzled relationships. It was called the hard stop. I had never been a very good communicator, so what I would think in my head would not come forth from my mouth. My tongue gets tied, and everything comes out ass backwards. Knowing this, I am more of an action girl. Knowing actions speak louder then words, the hard stop just happened one day.

I trusted in my gut completely once I had made the decision, and I wasted no time getting going. I usually jumped into relationships with both feet, so I decided the same was appropriate heading out the door. I put the house before the plan, sort of, and let the rest work itself out.

Once emotionally finished and the turmoil in my head subsided, I celebrated over a bottle of fine red wine. That was when my "super-powers" were most in tune with my emotional needs, and I made my plans. My gut told me the truth every single time, even if it was not what I wanted to hear. I would reflect on my epiphany, put on my big girl panties, and go out and buy a new house.

Once my ducks were lined up neatly in a row and plans were made, I would return home and deliver the news. In both cases, I felt like I had taken control of the situation, which was a pretty darn good feeling. Neither of these men were abusive or treated me badly, so leaving was harder because of it. I was a waffler and couldn't seem to untangle myself decisively. It was much like ripping off a band-aid or jumping in a cold lake. The slow way hurts more.

This was also my fail-proof way of not getting talked back into the failing relationship I was fleeing. I am a bit of a softy, so I took such large steps out of the relationship right from the start that there was no going back.

That technique really built up my courage. I was a little less afraid after that of going in, knowing that I had to practice going out and that I was capable of taking care of myself.

Changing your status to single is not all roses and sunshine, and I realize that. It is the unknown, after all. And if you don't go by, feel, how do we know if it is really the better side of the situation you currently reside in? If it is the right decision, you just know, and you choose better for yourself next time.

This is not to suggest that at the first sign of discontent, you up and relocate your life, but rather if you already know, skip the waffling, be brave, and get on with it if that is what your gut is telling you to do.

Life is short. Life is precious. Love yourself first and do what is best for you. Live to the best of your ability, love fiercely, and never apologize for doing it your way.

Julie Fairhurst

Never miss an opportunity to sit with yourself and your thoughts, appreciate your loved ones, and tell them how much you love them.

"The most critical time in any battle is not when I'm fatigued, it's when I no longer care."

Craig D Lounsbrough

Chapter 4

Sometimes, You Have No Other Choice

Theresa Waugh

"When I hear somebody sigh, 'Life is hard,'
I am always tempted to ask, 'Compared to what?'"
Sydney J. Harris

Twenty years as a stylist has taken a toll on my body, so when I wanted to change what I was doing but stay in the same industry, I went back to school to become an instructor for hairdressing. I had all this experience and knowledge to give back to the next generation of stylists.

I worked very hard to get my dream job. I was helping the next generation of hairstylists learn and achieve their goals and dreams. I was working at a very reputable school in downtown Vancouver and traveling one hour there and one hour back to work, but I loved what I was doing and did this for three years.

I wanted to work closer to home, and the opportunity came to work at a school near my home. I felt welcomed by all the staff, and they were all women. Three months in, I knew what was promised to me would not be fulfilled, and other issues I had were not being taken seriously.

During a staff meeting with three other co-workers, I heard a very offensive comment about my culture and a coworker's culture, there was also a minor present during this meeting who was also offended by the comment. I couldn't believe this was said at all and that they were more concerned about the government making a holiday for what was going on with missing children and the reconciliation day.

After the meeting, all the coworkers and the office manager discussed the racial comments and how offended we were, but nothing came of the complaint. When I started at this school, I originally thought I was in a safe place with a group of women to empower me and succeed. This was not a safe place. When I talked to coworkers and management about issues, problems, and concerns, it was left there and not looked upon to take it higher up.

The office manager had not helped with my concerns and told me we could go to the owner. When I eventually started standing up for myself and my rights, it was unwelcome and challenged. I felt trapped, unheard, and unsafe. I felt pressured to do as you were told and not to ask questions like a good employee.

With no resolutions and no one further to help with my concerns and issues not being addressed or handled, I was constantly being compared to a past employee who was retiring, and I was taking over. I felt defeated, worthless, undermined, less than. I had no choice but to give up my dream job and all my hard work.

Since I left that school, I have been unable to find another instructing position. I couldn't return to instruct at the very reputable place I left as they had closed down. I miss what I was giving to future stylists and teaching them.

All my hard work has gone over the way this company has treated their employees and their racial comments. I am trying to build up my self-confidence, get another instructing position, and be secure.

These positions are very rare and not something to leave, but I knew I had to stand up for what was right.

I also pray not to be treated or feel like this at a place of employment. There should be someone to turn to and feel safe. There needs to be something more a person can do to be protected from this in the future.

My children are very proud of me for what I did and for standing up for what is right. I will continue on my journey with teaching the next generation of stylists, but it will be God willing in my own school. I will open my own business and treat everyone with respect and dignity.

We never know the background of other people. My children and I have been through two generations of genocides. May our ancestors guide and protect us.

"Let us not hesitate to surrender to our desire and our passion for joy when we are willing to be reborn from the ashes of a lost past and feel ready to burn down desperation and boredom."

Erik Pevernagie

Chapter 5

Surrender to the Spirit Within

Donna Fairhurst

"Trust the dreams for in them is the hidden gate to eternity."
Kahill Gibran

Like everyone on Earth, I am an extraordinary Soul with a seemingly ordinary human experience that we call life. I AM the Chief Evolving Officer of Soul Full Solutions, an Intuitive Life and Soul Transition Coach, Reiki Master, Psychic Medium, Empath, Angelic, Auric, and Chakra Intuitive, Speaker, and 5 X Best-Selling Author so far.

None of this has been a cakewalk. My life has sometimes been very easy and, many times, gut-wrenchingly hard. Those hard times felt soul-destroying. I've had to dig deep and surrender to the experience of pain mentally, physically, emotionally, and spiritually.

More than once, lonely and in the depths of despair, I contemplated ending all. Fortunately for me, at those times, I was divinely protected by my angels, spiritual guides, and loving friends who literally drove me to seek help that saved my life.

Along the journey, I surrendered to live through and learned from near blindness, polio, cancer, a congenital heart condition, three near-death experiences, multiple failed relationships, losing two babies, two divorces, bankruptcy, multiple careers, and home transitions, traveling the world and rediscovering myself every step of the way.

I AM a Soul, a wife, a daughter, a sister, a mother, a grandmother, a friend, a neighbor, and a stranger. I feel, in some way, I cannot define that I AM every woman anywhere. I've been a student, clerk, banker, traveler, coach, teacher, friend, home saver, home wrecker, lifesaver, life destroyer, life-giver, healer of myself and others, and a few times my own and others' worst enemy.

Eventually, these experiences led me to the center of my being and my soulmate, Frank. It was Frank who consistently encouraged me well into my sixties, to discover and define what I was born to do finally.

I AM here now to share my journey through coaching, motivational speaking, and writing like this. My human journey has led me to define and refine myself every step of the way. I had to finally trust my intuition and lean into Creator/ God/ Spirit to discover and surrender what that means to me, not what others thought I should or could be. The challenge was/is always to surrender! To live from my life lessons, find purpose in the lesson, and forge my pathway to and through the light. To be ME and as perfectly imperfect as life is.

I AM I = INTENTION, INTELLIGENCE, INTUITION, and INSIGHT

A = AWARENESS, ALIGNMENT, and ACTION

M= MANIFESTING MAYHEM, MAGIC, and MIRACLES

Surrender is not about being either a victim or a hero in your own or other's lives. It's about the BEING of being HUMAN!

H = HOLY IN SPIRIT

U = UNBROKEN, UNDERSTANDING, and UNSTOPPABLE

M = MASTER/MISTRESS OF MANIFESTING

A = ALIVE, AWAKE, AWARE

N = NEW EVERY DAY EVERY STEP OF THE WAY

Choosing to "SURRENDER" on every level of our unique human experience is our spiritual journey. It does not mean giving up on you, your life, your family, or your purpose for BEING!

It means living from and shining your light upon the world from your unique experience to create calm and coherence rather than chaos and incoherence. To resonate at your highest level from the vibration of love. My life and near-death experiences have taught me that all there is on the other side of Human Beings is LOVE.

Eternal, never-ending, all-encompassing LOVE!

S = SEE U = UNDERSTAND UNITY WITH ALL THAT IS

R = REALITY R = RELEASE and RESTORE

E = EMBRACE and EXPRESS

D = DEFINE DOING VS BEING. BE WHO YOU ARE NOT WHAT YOU DO

E = ELEVATE ENERGY, EMBRACE, EXPRESS

R = REALIZE, REALIGN, RENEW, and REBIRTH.

All of this ably equipped me with a PHD in life, and what I describe as a human BEING a Yoyo to Creator/God/Creator. I was led, sometimes forced by my experiences, to study spiritual and healing modalities and practices for over four decades to discover who I really am.

I surrender to and choose to embrace and embody the highest degree of awareness I have at any given moment. I live to create the vibration of healing, first for myself and then for others via Reiki, Chakra, and Auric resonance.

In doing so, I share my always and ever-increasing psychic awareness. By combining life coaching, psychic and healing abilities, scientific aura imaging, and more, my purpose is to empower myself and others to pivot powerfully through any transition or challenge and create "SOUL FULL SOLUTIONS."

May we surrender to and reach our highest level of personal awareness, Balance, Clarity, and Coherence in the time and in the space we are choosing to BE HERE NOW!

Namaste Donna Fairhurst

"I wonder if pain comes from surrendering or resisting?"

Donna Lynn Hope

Chapter 6

Seat 1A The Queens Seat

Heather Scott

"There are no wrong turns, only unexpected paths."
Mark Nepo

Embracing the unknown means approaching unknown circumstances with an open mind. I am visual, so the unknown is out of my wheelhouse.

I am a work-acholic, "a person who compulsively works hard and long hours". Yikes, as I type that out, I feel like my picture should be next to the definition, lol.

Two things that come out of my mouth regularly is "I'm not a world traveller" and "I live vicariously through my customers." Over the last few decades, my Scottish Cousin Wendy and her husband Jim have come to Canada and stayed with me, usually around their anniversary. Wendy's Brother Keith and his wife Gail also came on their last visit. Then Jim's health took a turn, and the travel medical insurance outweighed the cost of coming over.

Now, taking a trip to Scotland has been in the back of my head for 30-plus years. Why do today what you could put off until tomorrow or 30 years? Lol, it was always a thought that ended up on the back shelve of my mind.

When it looked like they would not be able to return to Canada, I dusted off the thought, and it consumed me. Again, I'm not a world traveler; to say I know nothing is an understatement. I started reaching out to friends who visit Scotland regularly for advice.

Jokingly, I said to one of them that since I have never taken a vacation, I think I will book a first-class ticket. She laughed and said that it was really expensive, that she had just got a quote, and it was going to be $15,000.

Remember that back shelf; that is where that thought went. I asked another friend who goes all the time who he flew with, and he told me KLM explained the layovers he had and where. I went on to KLM and mocked up a Business Class return ticket using his layovers, etc.; sure enough, it was $15,000. So I "back shelved it."

Over a few months, I would go in and mock up the same dates and layovers and get prices as high as $16,000. In December 2022, I was speaking to the Former CEO of the company I work for. It is tradition that I email him every December to see how his year has gone and wish him a Merry Christmas.

We talked about my possible trip to Scotland, and he also gave me some advice and told me going First Class was a good idea (Covid and all). That night, I went home in the dark, sitting on the couch. I went onto KLM and mocked up the same trip I had mocked up several times before.

Same dates, same layovers, and all of a sudden, $15,000 dropped to $3600... "What?" Without even knowing if I would be approved for the time off, "SOLD." I requested the time off five months before I bought the ticket but had not heard anything.

I'm 63 years old, and other than the family vacations around British Columbia and Alberta, I really had not gone on what "other people" would call a vacation. I was doing/going alone and had no idea about anything; most of you probably think it is simple because you have traveled. I didn't know the ins and outs of the airports, security, etc.

Time started to fly by, and it was now seven months since I requested the time off, and still, I had heard nothing. Meanwhile, I continue to prepare for my lifetime trip, spending money and buying gifts!

I eventually got a call from my management team regarding my vacation request. You know the emoji that head explodes? Lol. Long story short, I said you have every right to decline my request, and I have every right to retire. "Explosion!" I could see the top of his lift-off. Wow, that could have gone the wrong way, but it was approved before we finished the call.

I started to get anxious; I had to release the fear of the unknown and embrace vulnerability. Acknowledging my fear and vulnerability and stepping into the unknown can be scary, and it's okay to acknowledge that fear. Recognize it and accept it as a natural reaction to something unfamiliar. That sounds like good advice; take my advice; I don't need it, lol.

The day had arrived, and I made my daughter and both my sisters come to the airport with me, thank goodness the airport is huge, and we were sent in different directions depending on who we asked. I'm checked in and now on my own, looking for the first-class lounge. (Which I found)

Now, the time has come to board the plane. I was in seat 1A. As I entered the plane, I told the Steward that I was in 1A, and he got all excited and said the "Queens Seat" and treated me like a queen; they absolutely did, including a visit to the cockpit and a picture with the pilots.

Fast forward to Amsterdam with no support system (huge airport). "Talk about Un-seen, Un-familiar, Un-certainty." Nothing, a good shot or two of Drambuie didn't help.

Staying with Wendy and Jim (familiar), I find it hard to say anything was the best part of the trip, but, let me try... What was unplanned and unexpected was that Wendy had been working on the family tree and got stopped at some point. When we got to her place she went and got the bag of what she had gotten done out.

She was stuck at our Great, Great-Great, and Great-Great-Great Grandparents. I said give me our great-grandmother's name; I input it into Google (my best friend), and within five minutes, we knew where they were buried. I have a picture standing next to a huge headstone at my great-grandmothers' and great-great grandparents' resting place.

Beautiful scenic country, breathtaking. Not being a world traveler, I am not a tourist, so to speak. I wanted to spend time with my family, meet the ones I had yet to meet and see the countryside, Highlands, and Lowlands. And I did see that and more 10-fold, could not be happier...

"Writing is both an act of power and surrender. Passion and discovery. It is a tug at your soul that continues to pull you forward, even as you go kicking and screaming."

Laraine Herring

Chapter 7

A Courageous Journey

Brenda Cooper

"Courage is grace under pressure."
Ernest Hemingway

A Courageous Journey

She dreams of a life without the abuse,
Where every day, she made an excuse,
She had surrendered her life to violent ways,
She would feel the pain and then the praise.

How can one live in a darkened place,
With tears and sorrow all over her face,
The daily fear, there is no escape,
The beatings, the bruises, and the rape.

Deep down she knows that she must leave,
Afraid of the unknown, she begins to grieve,
She is so reluctant to walk through the door,
As the outcome is bleak, she has been there before.

Julie Fairhurst

She feels the walls now that are closing in,
Dark thoughts are upon her, she cannot win,
Her life is worth something, this she does know,
She must find the courage, get up, and let go.

She has faced death by no fault of hers,
So many assaults that she just endures,
She thinks to herself the time has come,
She must fight for her life and not succumb.

She begins to fill her days with hope,
She writes down her thoughts, so she can cope,
She just can't surrender, not anymore,
She will be brave and step out that door.

When the sun arises, she finds her grace,
To accept the unseen, she dares to face,
In the morning glow, she finds her way,
A heart filled with courage, she will not sway.

With every heartbeat, she takes a step,
Into the unknown, she is not done yet,
There is a world out there, she is yet to see,
No turning back, she has set herself free.

She has finally embraced the unknown the unseen,
And the courage to surrender to her hopeful dream,
She will now walk a path that will light her way,
And remember this courage she had this day.

"Listen through your screams to the wind still whispering:
Don't give up -- Surrender!"

Eric Ganther

Chapter 8

Children Are From God

Sheron Chisholm

"What we really need is only a hurt to surrender and always trust what God has plan for our life. So we do our best, god shall take a rest. That's what I call Faith."
Olivia Sinage

I waited a long time, years. Ever since I can remember, I wanted to have children when I grew up. Then, I was thirty-five years old and single. I explored my options for adopting since I had no potential husbands in sight. I went to the agency doing adoptions in my city and found that they give adoptions to single women, but it was rare.

I decided to go ahead with the process of doing a home study and becoming approved for placement. Then I waited longer. In fact, I was moving to another city and decided to work with a different agency. This agency did place children in single-parent homes, but they were usually not babies or toddlers, which was my preference.

I waited longer, and then finally, I got a phone call from my case worker saying there was a thirteen-year-old girl available who the case worker felt would need a single-parent home. Did I want an

45

older child, or did I want to wait longer for a younger one? I decided to go and watch the video of the girl. It's the child that matters, not my wants, and if God brought her to me, there must be a reason.

This girl was well-spoken, tried to project maturity, and was direct and specific about what she wanted and did not want. The main points I picked up were that she wanted to be an astronaut or a lawyer, and she wanted a parent who would give her a home, clothes, food, and provide an education. She did not need a mother in the sense of emotional needs or decision-making because she had overseen herself her whole life and felt she could be independent.

Plus, she parented her younger brother and sister, whom I adopted later. I decided to surrender to God, to push the desire for a younger child, and to love this girl who had never experienced the love, caring, or attention from her birth parents.

She never had a chance to be a kid. I felt a nudge to go forward with adoption and meet this girl. I did adopt her; one year later, it was final, and she wanted to change her name to Kayla Nicole, after an actress on a daytime soap opera.

We had no instant bond, and I had to work very hard to establish my relationship with her. She was entering the eighth grade at a new school, so we did one of her favorite things: shopping. I invited my sister to go with us to meet Kayla and create a less tense atmosphere. My sister was more relaxed and completely different from me.

We got all the new clothes for school and some things for her room. Her comments about not needing a mother who was going to tell her what to do became a reality very quickly in our relationship. All I could think was, right now, what do I do? Here I am trying to work, have this new person staying at my house during the day, and try to have fun with her. I wanted to be home but could not because of our work situation.

She went ahead and decided and acted without discussing it with me, which was not appropriate. The worst part was she did not accept my explanation that it was inappropriate. Our first argument. I was learning that this adoption was going to be tough. There were going to be many times that I would have to give up my tendency to be in charge of everything, and there would be times when Kayla was not going to be as independent as she felt she ought to be. This was a challenge forever.

To compound this problem, she acted like she did not like my dog, Aretha. Eventually, Kayla told me she was jealous of the dog because she felt I paid more attention to Aretha than I did her. She wanted to be an only child. This became an important fact to remember.

Before getting to this point, I will add to the relationship that was an obstacle to becoming fully attached. I became more aware of my feelings when I first watched the video. That was that Kayla seemed a little closed off to discussion or sharing. She stayed direct and matter-of-fact when talking. I became more aware of this and how deep this behavior was as time went by. It was distressing to me because I wanted a close relationship with her in which we could freely discuss our feelings and concerns.

This happened to some degree, but not even close to what a mother-daughter relationship meant to me. Even as an adult, Kayla did not share most of the time unless asked, and then she shared only one small piece of the situation. This ended up being a surrender to accept what was and maybe would not become more. I wanted to have this great idyllic mother-daughter relationship I did not have with my mother, and she had not had with her mother. I wanted to enjoy life doing things together. That was not what was possible and probably not what God had in mind. I don't know.

On the more positive side, Kayla and I enjoyed traveling together, doing activities she had never done before, and she got to be the kid and do the things she missed. I felt proud of what we were able to accomplish.

One year before she graduated high school, I was asked if I wanted to adopt her younger brother and sister, who had just become available. After discussing it with Kayla, I decided I would like to adopt Jesse and Katrina.

After we were all together, Kayla decided she did not want her brother and sister there because they required more of my attention, and she was not the "only child." Kayla joined the Navy after graduation but was soon home because of a medical condition.

She had my first grandchild, which was a joy, and I became more excited as they came to live with me for about eight months. I loved Kayla dearly to the extent that she allowed. I offered everything I could but felt guilty because I thought I had failed her.

I had to surrender this outcome. I wanted more, but this was what I could do. I gave her up to the Lord many times during her life. Only God could do the rest.

Kayla's life was short. She had an inherited disorder that shortened her life at the age of 47 years old. She is in the Lord's hands now. I love and miss her every day.

"If all of the steps of surrender are present, then a great Rembrandt or Monet will evoke love because the artist is simply there in all his naked humanity."

Deepak Chopra

Chapter 9

Courage In The Face Of Adversity

Sheri Godfrey

"She was unstoppable, not because she did not have failures or
doubts, but because she continued on despite them."
Beau Taplin

In the tapestry of life, there are threads of resilience woven through
the fabric of our existence. These threads are not always visible, but
they hold the power to transform us in ways we could never imagine.
Embracing the Unseen - The Courage to Change is not just a title;
it's a testament to the profound strength that resides within each
woman. It's about finding courage in the face of the unknown and
emerging from life challenges with newfound resilience, confidence,
and skills.

The courage to change comes from within, a deep wellspring that
flows even in the darkest moments. Life obstacles, like unexpected
storms, allow us to embrace the unseen and the unknown, compelling
us to forge forward and change. I've walked a path strewn with
hurdles, each one a test of my mettle, challenging me to confront the
shadows and emerge stronger on the other side.

One defining moment stands out—an ordeal that should have marked the end of my story. A major car accident sent us tumbling down an embankment, the world spinning as we rolled for what felt like an eternity. Yet, here I am, a living testament to the resilience that lies dormant within us until adversity calls it forth. The wreckage became a metaphor for the rebuilding that would come—a reconstruction not just of the car but of my spirit.

Life's journey took me through the tumultuous waters of a volatile divorce, a legal battlefield, that spanned over a decade. Courtrooms became familiar territory, and each year brought forth new challenges to overcome. Yet, in the crucible of adversity, I discovered an inner strength I never knew existed. Resilience became my armor, and with each courtroom skirmish, I honed the skill of standing tall in the face of adversity.

Then, there was the night when the shadows came to life, and the line blurred between the seen and the unseen. An ex lurks in my living room's darkness, a chilling reminder that danger can wear familiar faces. That night, I learned the importance of self-preservation and the courage to create boundaries, even in the spaces we call home.

My home became a fortress under police watch—a circumstance I could never have anticipated. Life's script took an unexpected turn, and I navigated uncharted territory. But in those moments of uncertainty, I discovered the true essence of resilience. Adversity, in all its forms, became the catalyst for change, transforming me from meek and mild to strong and unyielding.

It's easy to feel defeated when life takes us on an unplanned detour, but it's in those detours that we often find our true selves. Though unnerving, the twists and turns in the road have the power to reshape our destinies. The unpleasant journeys, with their rocky terrain and steep climbs, lay the foundation for the most remarkable endings to our stories.

Resiliency, confidence, and new skills are born in the crucible of life's challenges. These are not bestowed upon us; they are earned through the trials that test our limits. The woman who emerges from the storm is not the same as the one who entered it. She is forged in the fire of adversity, refined by the pressure of life's challenges, and sculpted by the unseen hands of fate.

So, when adversity comes knocking, be ready to veer. Embrace the twists and turns in the road, for they are the threads that weave the intricate tapestry of your story. The courage to change resides within you, waiting to be awakened by life's unexpected moments.

Embrace the unseen, for it is in the shadows that you will find the strength to redefine your narrative and emerge as the resilient, confident woman you were always meant to be.

"Don't try to solve all your problems at the same time.
You really can't.
Instead, surrender to the flow of Life."

Avis Viswanathan

Chapter 10

Cancer Was How I Learned My Lullaby

Rhonda Devlin-Gilbert

"Angels are the guardians of hope and wonder,
the keepers of magic & dreams."
Unknown

Now, I don't necessarily want to go into the whole grueling journey of my cancer treatment but more so the energy around it and how I accidentally let it change my life, my way of being in my heart, and my soul.

The day I was told I had cancer, I told myself two things. One was, "I'm not going to die." And weirdly, this was a simple, calm statement I said to myself. "We're going to fight this, and we're going to win. No other outcome will be accepted."

No, I didn't truly understand the kind of battle I was in for, and there were days when I truly questioned my sanity. There were days when I wanted to quit, but I just kept on, alternating between living in the moment and sinking down into the pain to try and overcome it.

This is a great paradox, one of many that I have learned. What I didn't know then was that I was doing a form of meditation, more specifically, a form of transcendental meditation. And this can be applied to any pain or hurt in your life.

One way of releasing it is to sink down into it, immerse yourself into it fully, feel it for all it's worth without the emotion, and allow it to float around and through you and now the magic happens. It's like a strange lullaby; if you let it ~ it will sing you to a place of healing.

At first, it's very intense because it's painful; it's something that is hurting you, frustrating you, angering you, and then little by little, it becomes something that just is, and that's okay; it's in this moment that you can start to rise above it and distance yourself from it. Sometimes, and really most times, the process needs to be repeated. But when you experience it fully, it then allows you the freedom to let it go.

In fact, that is the purpose of sinking down into the fire of pain. Rather than resist or fight it, sink into it to let it burn out and allow new growth to begin.

The second thing I started on that day was a gratitude journal. No, this is not a new concept by any means. I had heard of gratitude journals, and at first, my attitude was yeah yeah I am thankful for everything blah blah blah. But on that day, when I was told death was a possible outcome (even though I decided it wasn't an acceptable outcome), I thought, "I have taken life for granted for far too long." Now was a time of being grateful for what I had.

These journals transformed my life! It made me look at my life right now and how much I had. It made me scrutinize my heart, my soul, my purpose, my feelings, all of it. It helped me to forgive, and it helped me to release so much toxicity and negativity that I didn't even realize I was using them as fake props of strength and success. My disillusioned and foolish concepts and ideals came crumbling down. I was being smashed, destroyed, and shattered on all levels. I was truly wrestling with my demons, who felt like they were on all sides of me.

I lost friends, I lost energy. Weirdly, I didn't lose my hair - it thinned, but I didn't lose it, And I didn't lose hope. I came to hope as if my life depended on it, and it probably did. I let hope wrap its arms around me to hold, rock, and sing to me the song of continuing on.

The Angel of Hope saved my life! At one appointment, I remember my doctor saying that the main reason I was winning this battle was my fighting attitude! Yes, but my strength came from my Angel, who was constantly there to sing my battle song for me. My Fight Lullaby. Music has great power ∼ my Fight Lullaby is what gave me the strength to carry on.

It also gave me the wisdom to know when to stop resisting and allow the healing to happen, and most importantly, it gave me the comfort that healing and living were a possibility. And that's all hope needs; it is the possibility. Cancer was my 180. It was the universe slapping me upside the head - hard. And as humans, we sometimes need those slaps.

Before all of this, I was becoming a person I wasn't liking. I was becoming hard of heart, demanding, uncompromising, desperate, and angry - I was always angry. And it was tiring me out. I wanted to and often did, blame others for the things going wrong in my life. I felt bitter, hurt, and betrayed. And with its mighty force, the universe stopped me dead in my tracks (no pun intended). And I am so grateful that it did. I am grateful for the journey of my illness, treatment, and surgery.

I am extremely grateful that I was taught how to tap into the universe's music, the angels' symphonies, and the lullaby of hope and healing.

"The moment of surrender is the moment you choose to lose control of your life, the split second of powerlessness where you trust that some kind of "higher power" better be in charge because you certainly aren't."

Bono

Chapter 11

Life Can Be So Confusing

Guelda Redman

"When surrender happens, the universe itself becomes your Guru
and starts walking you to your blissful home."
Shunya

The hardest part I have found is dealing with everyone else's expectations for me. Expectations are tough enough when they are from ourselves, but brutal when we take on other people's expectations. At some point in our lives, we should feel accepted for who we are. At some point, we ought to be able to take time to figure out who we are and what we want.

No pressure, outside influence, veiled comments, or sideways glances. We all deserve to meet the person that we are and learn to love ourselves for that. Outside pressure can make us decide things for ourselves that we choose because of someone else rather than ourselves, and life is spent feeling out of place. We rate the success of our lives based on whether we achieved what we believed we could, not on whether we listened to ourselves and are living the life that we feel led to live.

Instead of living someone else's expectations for you, wouldn't it be amazing to live your own?

The problem I have found is that even if you endeavor to live your own life, you will be met with comments, suggestions, and other people's insights that they feel the need to share. Men are under the assumption that they should be the main "breadwinner" in the family. Notice that the word winner implies that this is an end goal. They are expected to work towards a fulfilling career. There are assumptions that they should be handy around the house, be athletic, and like beer. Okay, that may all sound ridiculous, but that is the point. Why would it be wrong for a man to decide not to marry, be a stay-at-home parent, or be more artistic, craftier, and like wine?

Women are under the assumption that they must want to be married, be a mother, have a career, and be amazing at it all. We can cook, clean, grocery shop, garden, and have our kids in all of the obligatory events. We will remember all meetings, appointments, birthdays, and anniversaries. Ensure all our kids go to university and be "successful" themselves.

Do you assume if you see a woman who has a career and is not married that, she is missing out on something? Why? We don't live in the land of Hallmark; we actually live in a world of endless possibilities, but we hear comments, and then FOMO hits. Fear of missing out makes us wonder if they are right. Makes us second guess that we know ourselves best. Makes us compromise our own agenda to try to fit in even just a little of what everyone else expects.

There are expectations that we will want to travel, hit the top of the company, have a large show home, and drive a new car. All those things in our society mean "success." What about being happy? What about focusing on being who YOU were meant to be rather than what others expect? What about being okay with accepting the fluidity of needs and wants and not thinking that because you chose something at one time, and that time ends, and you move on to something else, the first thing was a mistake?

I hear often that people were "called" to something and then it doesn't necessarily work out, so they think they must have been wrong. Maybe you completed the task that was necessary for you. Maybe you were only meant to be there to contribute or learn something for a while. Be okay with change and know that your journey is not a straight line on a flat road but rather a windy one with hills and valleys.

As a motorcycle lover, those windy roads are what make the ride so much more interesting and fun. Not being able to see around the next corner is a step of faith that you need to follow if you are walking a path or riding that you feel led to.

So, what does that all mean for us? It means that it is difficult to navigate and live our own lives, but we have to trust ourselves and ask those around us to trust us. Mistakes or missteps are never the end, but rather just part of the journey, part of a learning process we all need to go through.

Surrendering ourselves, placing trust in our own instincts, and listening to our own mind, body, and soul is where we grow and blossom. Surrendering to what you know you were meant to do and be and turning off the voices around you is hard, scary and the fear of failure is what makes so many of us stay.

Some of those voices are loving, some are controlling, and some are hateful, and no matter which of those they are, it is equally hard to stop listening and start feeling and trusting your own thoughts and feelings.

My story? I wanted to go to college and have a career because I thought I would be better at that, but only the boys in my family went to university. Instead, I got married, had kids, and stayed home with them because I felt/heard that was the best thing to do for them.

It took me 20 years to get the tattoo I always wanted. It took me 35 years to learn to ride and buy a motorcycle. I hate to cook, but every time I think I can quit, someone moves back home, and I accept the responsibility to do it because I am Mom. I want my own business and to build my own form of success, which would be helping others grow and find success in their businesses, but if anything gets pushed aside when something or someone else needs help, it is me and my dreams.

I think we, as women, do that. I think that it is very hard for us to put ourselves and our dreams first. I'm still hoping and praying for the strength to surrender to myself and not others.

The one thing I did do...."I kept my own last name when I married. I kept my identity, and that means the world to me. Your life, it is worth risking everything to make it yours." Oprah.

"Surrender to your unruly nature and watch the miracles grow all around you."

Kris Franken

Chapter 12

Surrender In Death And Dying

Trish Scoular

"The hardest part of having faith
is not believing but surrendering."
Maharishi

Surrender in letting go comes from having faith in the process—a belief in something greater than yourself that gives you the strength to cope and carry through. I learned about surrendering from my work as a Continuing Care Assistant for 24 years. Working with the elderly as they slowly faded away. Either from a long illness, cancer, dementia, or Alzheimer's. Timeless and weathering!

The unknown, the abyss, is stranded in a dark tunnel as the light slowly fades away, as does your body, mind, and soul, leaving only a vessel that carries this life. A person born into a world that brought meaning, whether good or bad it was, is what they knew. Whether their life made sense to me didn't matter; what did was acceptance and finding ways to bring love and light into their life, bringing some moment of pleasure in their long fight.

I never fully understood death until I started working in this field of work. It is a complete and full acceptance of surrendering! Letting go and dying, how does one process that knowing they will no longer be on earth, where do they go when they die, how does spirituality or lack of impact, will they see their family again?

Seeing someone you have just given a bed bath to take their last breath is something so profound you can't actually put it into words. When their spouse felt their last day was now, it was not what they were expecting when they pulled into the driveway not mentally prepared to face it. It takes its toll and certainly doesn't help to feel vicarious trauma after so many years of working in the field that my own parents started getting sick.

Every time I talked about getting out of that field, they seemed to make me feel like I had to stay; it's a good job, and what's wrong with seniors? I am grateful for the job. I would tell them I want a change, to try something else. I was good at the job and smart enough to pursue higher education that would open more doors.

And I did become a Counsellor, a published author, and more, leaving my parents proud of what I had become and my achievements.

My greatest lesson in death and dying has come from watching my Mom. I don't think it matters whether they go fast or slow. It's the pain of it that is similar. Our mothers, who are best friends and sounding boards on the other end of the phone, whose advice we wanted and often didn't like what they said, while other times it was spot on and supportive.

Now she is sick, both my parents are! My Dad has congested heart failure, kidney cancer, and advanced Parkinson's, and my Mom, who got sick and never made it back to baseline, is in total care and living two cities over from my Dad, where they both were before all this happened.

I quit, packed up, and moved closer. The thought of not having them was emotionally exhausting; the dynamics with my siblings and learning from my Mom on letting go was what helped me process and accept the inevitable.

As I was sobbing and feeling left out and helpless not having a family of my own, was when my Mom would share her own feelings of not seeing everyone as she did every day, on FaceTime or on trips to visit one another. Now, she was helpless and in a wheelchair, having people bathe and feed her. But she had to come to that place of acceptance, knowing how her life had changed and how we, as a family, never thought we would see Mom end up in this way.

Yet in the surrendering and letting go, she has found joy and laughter as tiring as it can get; it's accepting what is. My Mom helped me come to that place of feeling I am not losing her but gaining the wisdom I need to get through and that when she does go, I will have succeeded in creating my own life, knowing all that time that she was close.

I realized that we are not selfish in wanting her to stay; perhaps that is the gift in walking this journey together now and till the end.

"Surrendering is better than suffering."

Garima Soni

Chapter 13

I'm Not Ready For The Cats

Brooke O'Connor

"Life is, most of all, about love - follow your heart, live out your dreams, smile, be happy, see the good in everyone you meet, and rise above those who try to make you feel low. Fill your heart and fill your soul - love, no matter what is always the answer."
Emma Heatherington

My man picker was broken, and here I was, over 40 and single again. At what point does one give up? At what point should I relinquish the idea that love was meant for me and decide to die alone and collect a clowder of cats for companionship? Where does one find a man who has high moral values, wants to live a decent life and isn't rife with sexual deviancy?

I couldn't stomach a drinker, so the bars were out of the question. The idea of hanging out at Home Depot and asking for help from handsome strangers seemed desperate. So, I turned to the internet. The pickings were slim, and after a few misguided meetings with men who pursued me with gusto, I called the less intense but kind and peaceful man on my list.

We spent some time talking and arranged a safe Sunday afternoon coffee date. The four hours at Starbucks was a list comparison. We went back and forth with critical points and important issues. I like this, I don't like that. I believe this, I don't believe that. He was checking off all my boxes.

He didn't try to manipulate me into a sexual encounter. He didn't even try to hold my hand. It was such a relief after the trauma of conversations I'd been having online. The previous encounters with men were highly sexual, slightly creepy, and sometimes devastating.

The policeman wanted to know what I would do to him sexually if I found him drugged, tied up, and unconscious on the couch. The baseball player wanted me to wear short skirts and high heels at all times, although I never wore either. The corrections officer told me what a gentleman he was, yet when we met for a walk in a park, he couldn't keep his hands to himself. Then there were the scammers, the losers, and the straightforward sex addicts.

Starbucks man was a breath of fresh air after all this. He went to church, wanted to be married, and was a man of fidelity. I convinced myself that these were the most important things. I explained to my adult children that love was a chemical storm of hormones and neurotransmitters that were not to be trusted. More importantly, there are shared values and a decent sense of what life should look like. People grow to love each other, as proven in many arranged marriages. I was ready for some safe, sane, peaceful years with a man who would not cheat or rock the boat.

About a year and a half later, we were married. I should have listened to that still, small voice inside me. I should have noticed how the water was getting hotter and hotter and jumped out of the pot before it started boiling. Yet I was determined. This marriage was going to work. I was never going to get divorced again.

I told myself I needed to adjust. No one is perfect- I certainly wasn't- and I needed to learn to bend and be patient. It took only one year for the smothering lack of love, affection, and consideration to start taking its toll. I got sick.

Doctors couldn't tell me what was wrong. Stress was all they could deduce. As time went on, I felt very close to dying. Yet, every time, I would find something to pull me up and try to focus on the good things until I discovered our strange marital dynamic.

When I was sick, he was happy. He brought me food and told me to put my feet up and watch TV. He didn't expect me to do anything but feel better. That sounds wonderful, but he wasn't happy when I was feeling better. His greatest depressive episodes and most miserable times were when I was trying to pull myself up. Sometimes, I would give up and return to bed to keep the peace.

Years went on, and this push-and-pull was on rotation. I tried to pull him up with me, and that didn't work. His lows kept getting lower, and his highs became almost nonexistent. My efforts to rise above current affairs provoked anger, discouragement, and pushback. Anything good, anything positive or moving forward, was initiated and orchestrated by me. I had to wrap every idea, plan, or purchase with cotton balls and soft blankets to soften the blow of his reactions.

Daily interactions were exhausting. Nothing made him happy, and I couldn't be happy trying to modify every breath into something he wouldn't overreact to. There came a point when I thought he was dealing with early Alzheimer's. I couldn't rationalize the radical behavior, irrational fears, expectations, and inconsistencies any longer.

I encouraged him to seek professional help, and through research, he discovered the key to his lifelong struggle with relationships. He was a high-functioning autistic. His brain will never change, but his behavior could if he wanted it to. I followed the counselor's advice, we separated, and I got counseling myself. According to our counselor, if my husband were going to change, now would be the time. He would have to want it bad enough to do the work.

Instead, he collapsed into a self-indulgent puddle of helplessness. He blamed me for his lifelong impotence in business and inability to function as a grown man in society.

I was now at an impasse—the forever vow vs self-preservation. It wasn't lost on me that within 48 hours of him leaving, I started to feel better. I knew this relationship was literally killing me. I also saw how nothing mattered to him except his miserable state, and he did nothing to change it, to win me back. He did nothing. I had to eat crow from seventeen states when I told my kids I was getting a divorce.

They were sad for me, but they never liked him anyway. He never created enough relational currency with them to matter. Church friends didn't understand because many of them had been in dysfunctional marriages for decades. I was alone and decided to save my life instead of making others happy.

They say we can only do as well as the tools we have. My tools were dull, rusty, and cracked. I had to buy new ones, mainly from the 3Cs: coaching, courses, and counseling.

Now, in my mid-fifties, I'm better prepared for anything in life. I certainly learned what I want and don't want. But I can tell you one thing: I'm not ready for the cats.

"Gratitude grows from the soil of letting go and surrender."

Donna Goddard

Chapter 14

100 Long Months of Surrender

Linda S Nelson

"Under the care of God's mighty hand,
we release the need to know when, why, and how."
Megan Evans

As far back as I can remember, I have always wanted to be a mom. And I wanted to have a BIG family! As the oldest child in a family of six children, I watched my mom maneuver, attending to each child in a chaotic household, and marveled at what she could do with all her littles wanting her attention - sometimes all at the same time.

Looking back as I observed all the happenings, I realize now I was destined to be in Human Resources and work with various diverse, unique people when I entered the workforce. I learned a lot about differences, personalities, perspectives, ways of responding, and behaviors -- all within that busy household unit.

I'm convinced that God had a plan! Somehow, I knew intuitively that being a parent and sending a child out into the world was the most important job you could ever have. It's not that my parents did a perfect job. There is no manual for how to parent correctly. And each child needs their own "customized manual" that a parent must learn about through trial and error.

What works for one child holds no guarantee that it'll be effective for another. I probably learned more about what NOT to do based on individual differences than what TO do in those early years. I often felt misunderstood and unheard in all the chaos.

Nevertheless, I grew up fascinated and curious about the differences in people. As I continued to observe the differences and the parenting responses in my mom and dad, I knew in the deepest parts of me that I was meant to be a mom. It was my destiny!

I went to catholic school, and it was always a big deal when we took part in the annual "Who wants to be a nun?" presentation. We were given a slide show and an exciting speech about the beautiful convent grounds and the peace-filled, abundant life of a nun. I distinctly remember the feeling of dread as they posed that infamous question at the end of the presentation each year by our special visitors. I tried to slink down as far as I could in my chair so they couldn't see the little girl who didn't want to be a nun - EVER! All the other girls raised their hands excitedly in the air when asked the question. Not me! I wanted to be a mom.

That always seemed like the higher calling to me. Fast forward to my college years where I met the man of my dreams - the man I could envision having a family with. He possessed many amazing qualities that I knew would benefit all my future children. So I said I would do it after finishing college and beginning my first year of teaching. We had been married for about three years and decided the time was right to start a family. We had good jobs, purchased a house, and felt ready! My dream of children was about to be realized. Life was good. I was so excited to start on what I considered my highest calling - the reason I was put on this earth.

It turned out that our decision to start a family was not that simple. Over the course of the next eight years of trying, we were just not able to get pregnant. We tried month after grueling month. Months turned into years. Eight long, painful years of my body telling us both that I failed - again. And again. And again.

Well-intentioned friends and family made hurtful comments that rocked us. Comments like - "You've been married a long time now. Isn't it time to have children?" "What's the problem?" Don't you want children?" Our friends and family who were expecting their own bundles of joy - stayed away -- or didn't tell us of their upcoming joy assuming we would not be happy for them because of being sad for ourselves.

That was so far from the truth about who we are as people. And it hurt deeply as that's what they thought of us. It was almost too much to bear. We HAD to hold on to hope. We needed to persevere despite the evidence that continued to mount that we might not realize our dream of building a family.

We struggled -- collectively -- and individually as we processed this huge void and deep pain in our lives. It wasn't easy to talk about, but we knew we needed to draw closer to each other and our faith. In short, we had to surrender. We had to trust that God wants to give His children the desires of their hearts -- that He would ultimately bless us with a child in His -- not our -- perfect timing.

We couldn't trust the evidence that proved itself out every month. We had to hold on to something deeper within -- that belief that we would someday be blessed with a child. We definitely couldn't see it - but we did believe it. We trusted God's plan and had to let go of our expectations as to how it would come about.

On June 11, 1985, after almost 100 long months of this painful roller coaster journey, we were blessed with our most prized possession - our only son. He is a stellar human being. We knew He was God's from the start, and we were chosen to be his parents. This assignment was not something we ever took for granted. We poured love into this amazing human, and now he and his soulmate have blessed us with our first grandchild -- a granddaughter -- who is as perfect and amazing as her father.

This, at one time, seemed an impossible dream, too. We'll celebrate her first birthday soon - and will thank God for the blessing of family and the gift of perseverance and trusting in His perfect plan for His children.

"Will you keep resisting the place you´ve been given, ignore the signs and find excuses for everything, just to get by? Or will you surrender to fate, trust your story and take your place so proud and sure that no one will ever doubt that that place was made for you and you only, like it in fact was?"

Charlotte Eriksson

Chapter 15

Embraced The Unseen, Leaned Into The Experience, And Surrendered

Dana K. Cartwright

"A heart of faith is anchored in the unseen." Bill Johnson

I believe there may be something wrong with Adam's hearing said the First Steps coordinator. I responded, "I wished it were that simple." I knew. I knew in my heart we were dealing with something bigger. "Ok, let's start with getting Adam's hearing checked."

Adam, our son, is a twin, and for the first 16 months of his life, he and his twin sister, Cali, reached milestones together. At 16 months, I noticed Cali gaining momentum then as she reached more milestones, Adam would reach the same milestones six months later. I shared with the First Steps coordinator a few of the behaviors Adam displayed- walking on his tiptoes, staring out the window during mealtimes, and not responding when his name was called. I believed Adam had autism.

Adam's hearing evaluation came back negative, as anticipated. That is when the First Steps coordinator stepped into gear, making plans for evaluations and providing a snapshot of our life moving forward.

Hectic, busy, controlled, unpredictable, and stressful were the words and emotions that swirled around me. I felt as if I couldn't breathe. The mountain that stood before us appeared enormous, and I felt our carefree days were no longer.

As I was told the next steps needed to be done, I felt my mind drift. Is this really happening? Am I strong enough to handle this? What exactly is this? What are my options? As I pondered these big questions, a thought occurred. Summer is upon us, and the First Steps coordinator was wrapping up at the end of the month, May, and returning in August. What if the twins and I also paused? I knew I was in for the long haul, and I knew once the process started, I was all in. I was a stay-at-home mom, and the thought of having the next couple of months be just us minus any evaluations, diagnoses, or therapists excited me! I could step back and envision my husband and I pouring even more love than we already had into these two tiny humans.

Just the four of us for a little while longer made my heart happy. I felt it would serve our little humans well, and I felt it would give me the time needed to process it all and time to build the mental strength needed in the very near future. I communicated our plans to our coordinator, promising to be present and ready in August. Her smile and nod were confirmation she approved. To this date, 16 years later, that summer is still one of my favorite summers spent with the twins.

August appeared, and as promised from the first meeting post-summer to this day, I am all in as Adam's voice and advocate. My first challenge was convincing our pediatrician at the time that Adam was showing signs of autism. "Oh, he is just a boy. Boys do not develop as quickly as girls" became a very familiar phrase from the pediatrician to the music class teacher to the Gymboree instructor.

Fortunately, Adam was a twin, so I had a built-in peer to compare. I was with these sweet 18-month-old toddlers day in and day out. I saw the differences all too clearly. The only person who listened and understood was our First Steps coordinator. She quickly became my lifeline, and the only way we could get others to hear us was to show them the Applied Behavior Analysis evaluation, Speech therapy, and Occupational therapy evaluations. I found it fascinating; I was with Adam 24 hours a day, seven days a week, and my opinion carried very little weight. As time passed, my voice became stronger, and eventually, I became a valued member of Team Adam.

Getting a valid diagnosis was first on the agenda. I clearly remember the experience. I was told the wait time for an evaluation to receive a diagnosis at the two major hospitals in our area was eight months to over one year. I was stunned; however, there was no way I would waste that time. With autism, you are constantly trying to beat the clock, as early intervention has the most promising outcomes.

Fortunately, we were placed on the waitlist, and within three months, a cancellation occurred, and we received the call to have Adam evaluated. My husband was traveling overseas at the time, and I had yet to fill out the 16-page packet required at the time of the evaluation. I had no idea how I would pull this off, but I knew in my soul I would not let this unexpected opportunity pass.

I called a trusted friend to come to our home to stay with Cali the next morning and stayed up until midnight, filling out the packet. Adam and I made it on time, made it through the four hour evaluation and at the end, a panel of five experts sat before me and told me our son has Autistic Disorder.

Although I knew in my heart Adam had autism, hearing the panel speak the words produced a flood of emotions I never expected. I remained composed, thanked everyone, and hugged my sweet Adam tighter than I ever had.

From that moment on, I embraced the unseen, leaned into the experience, and surrendered any negative thoughts. I asked for Divine guidance in our journey and listened to direction every step of the way. God continues to place amazing people in Adam's path, and each of our lives is enriched because of Adam's journey. I am grateful!

"Too often surrender is an option that exists only
because we created it.
And if that's so, is it really an option?"

Craig D. Lounsbrough

Chapter 16

Letting Go Is The Right Thing To Do

Grace

"When you let go of fear and the need to control, you'll experience
how mysterious, sacred, and interesting life can be."
Melody Beattie

Family brings with it many joys; however, it can bring a great deal of
pain and suffering. I grew up in a working-class family with five
siblings and a stay-at-home mom. Well, most of the time, she was out,
but she didn't work outside of the house.

Mom was a passionate, feisty lady although short in stature, her pres-
ence was always known. She could be warm and compassionate, even
funny on the one hand, and then fly off the handle, curse, and throw
things when something upset her. My father would reprimand us and
remind us to behave so that we didn't trigger her outbursts. I quickly
learned "how not to be" by observing my siblings and what they did
that threw mom into a rage.

I learned to be the perfect child, and although I was never the object
of my mom's wrath, I was never recognized for not doing anything to

add to the drama in the home. Instead, I observed, listened to, and paid witness to the chaos over and over.

In my twenties, I realized my mom had an undiagnosed mental health disorder. I brought it to her physician's attention, and she was diagnosed as having bipolar disease. Unfortunately, she didn't acknowledge the need for help and refused any medication for most of my life. The ups and downs in her behavior and the challenges of being her daughter were ongoing.

The perfect child syndrome became part of my identity and caused me my own share of agony. I made a profession out of helping others. When people asked for my help, I tended to take it more seriously than they did- I made their problem my problem. Worst of all, I tried to help others even when they didn't ask for help and would feel frustrated when it caused more harm than good. All of these created scars within my own psyche, and the cumulation of it caused me periods of burnout and severe stress.

I couldn't live up to these crazy standards I set for myself as a daughter, sibling, friend, wife, mom, and professional. I was unhappy and exhausted. The emotional and mental anguish was showing up in my physical body as hormonal issues, digestive issues, and inflammation.

Something needed to change, and I started to realize that it wasn't going to be the people or circumstances in my life, it was going to have to be me! Thankfully, I had the wisdom and courage to seek help. With a lot of soul-searching on my own healing journey, I came to discover that I was addicted to feeling responsible for everything and everyone.

The truth is that this was a form of control to fill the gap of never feeling connected, loved, or safe in the world. Sadly, the need for approval was attached to the weight of carrying everyone else's burdens. Of course, this approval never seemed to come, and the cost of receiving it was far higher than the reward.

When I learned this, I proudly made significant changes to how I perceived things and related to others. I learned to love myself and create healthier boundaries around what I would take on and how I would interact in my relationships. Things felt calmer and more peaceful as I started to trust in life more each day. I felt more abundant in all areas of my life until I faced another major challenge.

Individuals who have trauma often never fully close the loop on their survival responses- that sympathetic nervous system flight, fight, or freeze reaction to stress. So, when this challenge arose, it flipped the switch on and triggered the old patterns. I found myself faced with the hardest battle of my life as I tried to enact the new version of me- the one that surrendered the need to be responsible to and for others and who tried to control life in order to feel safe and deserving.

My mother had a major breakdown at the same time that another family member was making some very questionable choices that could only be explained by either a mental health crisis and/or combined drug addiction. Mental health is complicated and challenged my need for boundaries on levels I never dreamed possible.

Being in this situation caused the biggest moral crisis I have ever found myself in. By the very nature of the disease, these individuals need help, and yet, most often, they are the ones who will refuse help. The things they will expect and ask of you will require you to battle this internal feeling of wanting to help but really only enable the illness. Letting go of the co-dependency in the relationship makes you feel like a horrible, heartless person abandoning someone in their time of need. Yet, it is the very thing that is needed to bring any hope of recovery.

My boundaries were tested beyond imagination. I cried every day for three years as I tried to reconcile that what was the right thing to do felt terrible. The old me urged me to come to the rescue and make everything better for them and myself. If only they stopped, my life would feel safe again. I would feel at peace.

But that feeling stemmed from the need for control and was giving my power to them, to something outside of me. I had to create a feeling of safety and peace within me without the attachment to their mental health getting better.

People have to want to change; they need to want help, and even then, it is a long journey to put those changes into everyday living. Even people with mental health issues or addiction can choose to seek help, although it is hard for them, and many never do. This was the hardest thing in my life to let go of!

I still have to talk to myself daily and give myself permission and acceptance. Some days, I need to speak to my mentor, who reminds me that I am surrendering my codependent need to rescue others because letting go is the right thing to do and the only way I can find safety and peace.

"Sometimes the only thing you can do is accept the fact that there is nothing you can do."

Mokokoma Mokhonoana

Chapter 17

Every Moment Of The Unknown Was Worth It

Emily Cronk

"I'll love you forever, I'll like you for always;
as long as I'm living, my baby, you'll be."
Robert N. Munsch

Four weeks and five days is the amount of time I spent unable to eat, sleep, do basic care for myself, or enjoy life. Everything came up as fast as it went down: my stomach felt like I had eaten broken glass, my body ached, my hair fell out, my teeth fell out.

I would be soaked from sweating ten times a night, and my friends stopped coming around. I lost my job, and my relationship suffered. I was a skeleton at four months pregnant, 109 pounds.

I was growing a baby in my body and praying the baby would make it long inside of me to be compatible with life. I have always wanted to be a mother, but due to medical issues, doctors didn't see that happening for me, so I was scared but hopeful, to say the least.

Pretty soon, the doctor's appointments became weekly, emergency room visits every few days for fluid, iron infusions, and IV medication for nausea. I was then diagnosed with Hyperemesis Gravidarum.

Hyperemesis gravidarum is extreme, persistent nausea and vomiting during pregnancy. It can lead to dehydration, weight loss, electrolyte imbalances, and sometimes death. The condition can make it difficult to continue working or care for yourself. It can cause anxiety and depression in some women that lingers after the pregnancy, and some women even commit suicide.

Constantly, I was begging doctors to put in a feeding tube, keep me at the hospital, anything that would help us. I would pray to survive, for us to survive. Every day felt like a battle for both of our lives. I was sad, anxious, and afraid of what was to come, but I never gave up hope.

One evening, as I drifted in and out of sleep, my back was in excruciating pain. I felt a gush of fluid, and I sat up to another gush. I flicked on the light to discover myself covered in blood. I thought that I was dying. We hurried to the hospital. I was hooked up to all the machines, and I could see the tiny heartbeat going on the monitor, and for a second, everything stopped.

I thought to myself, "This is my family, this is my big moment, and I'm going to survive, and so is this baby." And we did. The baby came into this world at 9:49 pm, on a smoky night in July, almost six weeks early and ready to fight.

Screaming like the little warrior I hoped she was going to be. She was placed in my arms and settled immediately. Her eyes looked up at me, and I'll never forget saying to her as she held my thumb, "We made it!"

The sadness and fear melted away and were replaced with utter love for the baby and the family I made on my own. I was and still am so proud of myself for enduring one of the worst sicknesses I've ever faced, and I would face it again in a heartbeat. This little baby was worth it and more. It's not just being a parent that is the most meaningful for me; it's the journey we take, the love we choose, the moments we share, and the relationships we build that make us caregivers. Four years later, I did endure it all over again for my second daughter.

This is dedicated to my children, Violet and Avery. You make life so beautiful.

"True sensuality comes with an internal surrender compass and confession that hits far deeper than any lie you can ever tell yourself."

Lebo Grand

Chapter 18

Living In The Unknown And Trusting That The Universe Has My Back

Jules Hik

"The soul of the Universe awaits to enfold you in pure white light."
Earthschool Harmony

The Adventure of Cancun, Mexico: I have a friend, her name is Iris, but to me, she's always been Flower. She is an older version of myself. She is funny, speaks her truth, has a huge heart, and loves living life.

I like living in the unknown and trusting that the universe has my back. I was pondering a conversation about needing a holiday, and Flower had just had a hysterectomy. We were talking on the phone, and she said yeah, let's go somewhere. I am an amazing wizard at finding excellent prices to travel, so I found a cheap deal for $200 each for us to go within 24 hours, so the adventure was on.

I was able to get my dad to watch my kids; Flower came over the day we were leaving, and we went over our paperwork. She showed me her birth certificate, which was a photocopy, and I thought that was OK at that time. I didn't realize it was a photocopy, so we got on our plane, and Flower had a wheelchair because she was in pain after just having surgery.

Mexico, we arrived. Yahoo! While standing there, I gave the customs guard my paperwork. Then, the customs guard asked for Flower's paperwork. We handed the paperwork to the customs fellow, and he looked at it, and then he looked at me. He stated, "This is a photocopy."

I looked at Flower, laughing in my eyes! I asked her, "Is this a photocopy? She tells me yes. I then asked her, "Well, where is the real one? She tells me it's at home.

I look at the customer fellow like I'm totally shocked. I wait for a few minutes, praying silently. I then asked Flower to give me her wallet so that this guy could make a decision about whether we could come into the country or not.

I'm thinking, Oh my God, what am I gonna do? Am I gonna stay in Mexico? Am I gonna fly her back home? The Mexican border guard looks at me. He stamps our little card, and we can go into Mexico.

I was so overjoyed. What a miracle I handed him 20 bucks Canadian. I said thank you, and we walked away. I was laughing to myself, "Oh my God, is this how the adventure is going to start?

I didn't realize that it could have looked like I had bribed him by giving him money, but he had already made the choice.

We got to the hotel, and it was beautiful. We walk to the water. It is amazing. It's crystal blue. The sun is still out, touching our body just like a tender kiss.

At our hotel, we got familiar with our surroundings. I didn't realize how serious a hysterectomy was, and I made Flower walk and treated her like she was physically healthy.

We decided to start our journey to go to Playa de Carmen. Having no idea where we would end up, just trusting in life. We met two guys, and they led us to a little hotel. Flower was a wild card; we chatted and had a nice dinner.

Later, those two guys came back and found our room. I heard a knock and got up from bed, and they were at the door, so I let them in. To my surprise, when I climbed back into bed, one of the guys thought he was in luck with two women. lol, Hell no! He put his head under the sheets at the end of the bed and went for me. Well, that was a hell no for me. Then Flower was next. I know some people would be freaked out, but we found it funny. We just started belly laughing so hard we were crying in pain. Thanks for the offer. But no thanks!

The next day, we ended up going to Chichen Itza. There's a pyramid that you can climb. Flower was scared of heights. But, with the awe of how old these were, we took the opportunity. We climbed the pyramid. What a breathtaking view! I had done it a few years before, and Flower held on to me as we looked around in all directions. A memory never to forget.

Then, in my defense, I never thought about how we would go down the stairs. Flower was frozen. The easy part was going up. Now I'm thinking, how the hell do I get her down? I'm not carrying her. Remember, she is recovering from surgery.

So I had to coach her with her on the steps, and our asses took one stair at a time. She had to focus on my face, stop for breaths, and take her time. We made it down, and she was overjoyed with excitement as she faced fear.

Following my intuition of the unknown, we went to Playa de Carmen and found a place on the beach. We made sure to ask that they had hot and cold water, so we were excited to have a shower. Flower ran to get in first, and then I heard this scream. She is naked. and I had just taken my bathing suit off and ran in her. She's yelling no hot water! Well, that's when I had my first and ever golden shower; if you could have seen us laughing and trying to figure out the water. Picture it in your mind. I hope you can get the just of it. The conclusion was they had no hot water, only the hose heated up outside. It was a great lesson.

Later, we went out to have some fun and saw lights flashing like a disco; we decided to check it out. We met lots of people from all over the world. I was talking to a man who worked in Belize for the army, and he was from England. I mentioned some spiritual lessons I had learned that everything happens for a reason. There are no mistakes. And when emotional things happen, we must clear out of ourselves.

Why am I telling you this story? I found it very magical for me. He was married and had kids, and what I said to him shocked him as if god was speaking to him. Later, I found out he was taking a bus back to Belize, and at that time, they had found some new artifacts. He asked me to go with him to a big party and then fly back. Wink wink, he had no idea I really wanted to go to Belize as I had brought my passport, so god was speaking to me. I had two days left in Mexico and had to fly home. The bus ride was 15 hours, and then the party, then try to catch a flight home.

I declined the offer only because I didn't know if the planes would get me back in time. YES, we are talking about before Google, lol. Also, just to be clear, it was not a romance, just a traveling buddy. I guess you wonder what happened to him. I got a call from him, and he told me he made it to the party and was so grateful for our chat that he met another woman with whom he had a great conversation. He told me he felt things may have been different with this other woman if he hadn't met me and had our conversation. It was the power of God, the Universe, that he needed to have a wonderful experience.

Flower and I made it home. Her body healed faster because of all the walking, water, and sun—moments to cherish.

"Gratitude is a form of surrender. It is a way of saying: I am enough, I have enough, and my life is enough."

Vanessa Autrey

Chapter 19

Embrace The Mysterious And Unlock The Wonders Of The Unknown

Julie Breaks

"Today, I decided to let go. I let go of my grasp on people, things, thoughts, feelings, expectations, and outcomes. And though I acknowledge my desires, I acknowledge I do not control anything. Letting go activates my faith and allows God to send what is meant for me. Letting go helps me because holding on does not."
Emmanuella Raphaelle

My life has been full of the unseen, and I have had to trust the universe to "sort out" what has been best for me. Even when I was terrified of the unseen ahead of me, knowing there was no control over situations allowed me to let go and allow. And that has not been easy.

Being let go from an amazing job opportunity sent me into a dark hole. I cried for two days and was devastated. The unseen was terrifying. However, within a few months, I realized it was the absolute best thing that could have happened to me.

Julie Fairhurst

It gave me the perspective to jump fully into my sales career, and I killed it. I never would have made the money, awards, and success in my life and career if I had not been let go from that amazing job.

The fear of being a single mother at times was overwhelming. I made the decision to divorce the father of my three young boys. That was scary. The unseen before me was dark, and I experienced a lack of confidence and plenty of anxiety. Once again, though, it was the best thing I could have done.

I was a single mother for 24 years. It was super hard at times. None of us came out of those years unscathed. However, it was one of my best decisions. I have remarried, and my husband is wonderful. I don't know how we found each other, but it has been a life blessing for all of us.

Sure, it's easy to say there is something amazingly wonderful on the other side of the unseen. But while you are going through it, it's hard to believe that good will come out of it. I would say embrace change and trust your decisions and abilities to deal with life.

It can be a super exciting journey filled with personal growth and resilience! Opening our minds and hearts to the unknown, we pave the way for unexpected and extraordinary experiences. This adventurous spirit helps us break free from our comfort zones and take on new challenges in the outside world and deep within ourselves.

It's a constant reminder that life is full of incredible surprises, and when we give up our need for tight control, we become more flexible and receptive to the opportunities that come our way. So, let's embrace the mysterious and unlock the wonders of the unknown!

"In the moment of surrender, you are free."

Kris Franken

Part Two

Women Like Me Movement

"I Unconditionally Surrender to The Miracles of Life."

Ujjwal Arora

Chapter 20

Women Like Me Community

Join The Movement

The power of women's stories lies in their ability to inspire, challenge, educate, and connect. They are both a reflection of individual experiences and a testament to collective strength. In sharing and honoring women's stories, we can recognize the contributions, challenges, and diversity of women's lives.

Empowerment Through Unity - One voice can make a sound, but a chorus can shake the earth. "Women Like Me" is more than just a movement; it's a collective voice of women from different walks of life coming together to make meaningful changes in society. By joining, you amplify that voice and make it resonate even louder.

Shared Experiences - No matter our backgrounds, women around the world face similar challenges. By joining this movement, you get access to a wealth of shared experiences and insights that can inspire and guide you in your personal journey.

A Safe and Supportive Space - The "Women Like Me" movement offers a platform where your voice is not just heard but celebrated. It's a space where you can express yourself without fear of judgment and where your experiences are validated.

Opportunities for Growth - Beyond sharing stories, this movement provides personal and professional growth opportunities. Members can access resources to help them thrive in their chosen paths through networking, workshops, mentorship programs, and more.

Making a Difference - The stories in the "Women Like Me book series" aren't just narratives; they serve a larger purpose. By supporting this movement, you directly contribute to empowering women to care for their families.

Celebrate Womanhood - At its core, the "Women Like Me" movement is a celebration of being a woman. It's an embrace of our strengths, vulnerabilities, stories, and potential.

In essence, joining the "Women Like Me" movement is more than just aligning with a cause; it's a declaration. It says you believe in the power of women, in shared stories, and in a future where every woman has the opportunity to shine. Will you lend your voice, your strength, and your passion to this vibrant tapestry of womanhood?

Join Us Here:

https://www.facebook.com/groups/879482909307802

"The best way to achieve success in any area of life is to surrender yourself to it and you will get it."

Shiva Negi

Chapter 21

Women Like Me Book Series

Everyone has a story. And oftentimes, those stories can be powerful things that help us learn and grow. But for some people, their stories can be a source of pain. They may feel like they can't escape their past or that their story is holding them back from living their best lives.

If you're one of those people, know that you're not alone. And more importantly, know that there is hope. There are ways to turn your personal story into something positive and to find healing from the past.

One way is to share your story with others. This can be incredibly cathartic, and it can also help others who have been through similar experiences. you process your feelings and work through any trauma you may be carrying around. And finally, don't forget that your story doesn't define you. You are more than your history. You are more than your pain. You are more than your mistakes. You are more than your story. You are strong, you are brave, and you are enough. So don't let your story hold you back.

Writing about your past can be very beneficial, both emotionally and psychologically. You can increase your feelings of well-being and even improve your physical health. When you write about your past experiences, you relive them in your mind. This can help you to process difficult or traumatic events, and it can also provide you with some closure.

Additionally, writing about your past can help you to understand yourself better and work through any unresolved issues. It can also allow you to see yourself in a new light, which can be both healing and empowering. In addition to helping you emotionally, writing about your past can also be beneficial physically. Studies have shown that expressive writing can help to reduce stress, anxiety, and depression. It can also help to improve your immune system function and promote a sense of calm. So, if you're feeling stressed out or overwhelmed, consider picking up a pen and starting to write.

We only have one shot at this life, and it's our only shot. There are no do overs. There are no second chances. So, we better make the most of it. We only have this moment right here, right now, and it's the only moment that matters. We only have so much time on this planet and must spend it wisely. We only have so much energy and want to spend it on things that bring us joy. We only have so much love to give and want to give it to people who appreciate it.

A story is a powerful thing. It can draw you in, take you on a journey, and leave you with a lasting impression. That's why I love listening to other people's stories. Everyone has a story to tell, and I'm always eager to hear a new one.

Visit the Women Like Me Stories website at www.womelikemestories.com and get in touch. The world will be waiting.

Women Like Me Stories

https://womenlikemestories.com/tell-your-story/

"When surrender happens, the universe itself becomes your Guru and starts walking you to your blissful home."

Shunya

Chapter 22

Read More From Julie Fairhurst
And The Women Like Me Community

Books are available on Amazon or the Women Like Me Stories website.

Women Like Me Book Series

Women Like Me – A Celebration of Courage and Triumphs

Women Like Me – Stories of Resilience and Courage

Women Like Me – A Tribute to the Brave and Wise

Women Like Me – Breaking Through the Silence

Women Like Me – From Loss to Living

Women Like Me – Healing and Acceptance

Women Like Me – Reclaiming Our Power

Women Like Me – Whispers of Warriors: Women Who Refused to Stay Broken

Women Like Me – Embracing the Unseen - The Courage to Surrender

---

Women Like Me In Kenya

(100% of the book proceeds go directly to the 26 Kenya Authors)

Women Like Me – Strong Women in Kenya

Women Like Me – Journey Through the Eyes of Kenya Women

Women Like Me Community Book Series

Women Like Me Community – Messages to My Younger Self

Women Like Me Community – Sharing Words of Gratitude

Women Like Me Community – Sharing What We Know to Be True

Women Like Me Community – Journal for Self-Discovery

Women Like Me Community – Sharing Life's Important Lessons

Women Like Me Community – Having Better Relationships

Women Like Me Community – Honoring The Women in Our Lives

Women Like Me Community – Letter's to our Future Selves

Sales and Personal Growth

Transferring Enthusiasm - The Sales Book For Your Business Growth

Positivity Makes All The Difference

Agent Etiquette – 14 Things You Didn't Learn in Real Estate School

7 Keys to Success – How to Become A Real Estate Badass

30 Days to Real Estate Action – Real Strategies & Real Connections

Why Agents Quit The Business

Powerful Persuasion – Unlocking the Five Key Strategies for Business Success

"To surrender, to submit, it is enough."

Lailah Gifty Akita

www.ingramcontent.com/pod-product-compliance
Lightning Source LLC
LaVergne TN
LVHW052029080426
835513LV00018B/2242